NO DESIGN MANIFESTO

BIS PUBLISHERS

THEY WANT YOUR SHAME!

DESIGN BEYOND SHAME

ORDER NOWADAYS IS MOSTLY MET WHERE THERE IS NOTHING.

IT IS A PHENOMENON OF SHORTAGE.

Bertolt Brecht

CONTENT

Part 1

PART 2

PART 3

Part

MORAL IS FASHION

Concept & Design by Mieke Gerritzen based on
texts by Mieke Gerritzen, Silvio Lorusso, Geert Lovink,
Ned Rossiter, Koert van Mensvoort
ISBN 978-90-636-9807-2

There's a wonderful sign hanging in a Toronto junkyard which reads:

HELP BEAUTIFY JUNKYARDS.

THROW SOMETHING LOVELY AWAY TODAY.

Marshall McLuhan

SHAME YOURSELF TO BE A MAKER!

Shame is a powerful emotion that drains energy and joy. It makes us want to disappear, trapping us in a prison of self-doubt and isolation.

Contrechoc

Welcome to a world where everything seems "wrong": eating meat, smoking, crypto, data, campfire, whatsapp. Even your houseplant might be a climate offender. We're flooded with dos and don'ts, as if daily life must constantly be corrected by a moral authority. But what if we didn't shrink back in shame—but moved forward in imagination?

At Next Nature, we don't believe in going back to nature—we believe in moving forward. A nature where humans and technology co-evolve, not under strict rules, but through new forms of play. Design shouldn't be a moral compass—it should be a living system full of creative potential.

Instead of turning design into a lecture in good behavior, we see it as a space for radical curiosity. Not statements that neatly align with policy frameworks, but experiences that invite us to feel, think, and act. The future doesn't need perfection—it needs new connections—between nature and algorithm, bacteria and emotion, human and more-than-human.

Forget the checklist, embrace the eco-system. Don't fear the wild edges of the unknown. The new manual? We're writing it ourselves. Together. Through design.

IF WE
CAN SHARE
OUR STORY
WITH SOMEONE
WHO RESPONDS
WITH EMPATHY...
SHAME CAN'T
SURVIVE.

Brené Brown

FLOWERS BLOOM WHERE THEY HAVE SPACE, AND SO DO PEOPLE.

Phil Bosmans

DESIGN SHAME

In the design world, attention to social themes such as sustainability, ethics, and social responsibility has grown significantly in recent years. That is both valuable and necessary. Designers play an important role in thinking through the major questions of our time — from climate to technology, from health to justice.

But what activities or products have now ended up on the blacklist? No more meat. No alcohol. Sugar is taboo. Dairy and carbohydrates are bad for your health. Flying? Preferably not. Drive less. Skiing is wrong. Don't have children. Don't sit too much. Cut down on binge-watching. Delete Facebook. No TikTok. AI? The next digital disaster. No fast fashion. No more having packages delivered. Even a bouquet of flowers on the table or a barbecue has become suspicious.

Designers are increasingly expected to take responsibility. Policy frameworks, clients, and social norms push ever more strongly toward 'the right kind of design'. That can be inspiring, but it can also feel like a limitation on creative freedom. What happens if your work doesn't quite align with what society expects of you? Or when you're working on a project you have doubts about?

A quiet sense of discomfort — or even shame — is creeping into the field. A feeling that, as a designer, you must conform to a prevailing ideal. Those who don't focus on sustainability or behavioral change quickly find themselves on the sidelines. Yet it's precisely in the open space of creative freedom where imagination and innovation should arise.

Design sometimes seems caught in a double role: first contributing to consumption and growth, and then being called upon to 'repair' the over-consumed world. Rather than redesigning everything by the book, we could also look for new ways of thinking, making, and being. Not as a moral compass, but as an invitation to experiment, to imagine, to see things differently.

The shift toward socially engaged design offers many opportunities, but it also calls for a renewed appreciation of autonomy, curiosity, and experimentation. Designers don't have to just follow — they can also take the lead. By asking their own questions. By making space for doubt, for discomfort, for the unexpected.

And that may well be the greatest strength of design: not answering existing norms, but opening up new worlds.

TIME FOR A BROADER CONVERSATION

Perhaps some questions still feel too early. But for a good conversation — or a critical debate — it's never really too early. We live in a time of major change: rising polarization and inequality, alongside a growing need for meaning. In such a world, art and design matter.

But can the new generation of designers — raised with algorithms, social media, and constant stimuli — take enough distance to develop their own, free design vision? A vision that not only responds to the world but imagines new ones?

That also means designers must be able to say “no” from time to time. That they are given space to doubt, to not know, and to question whether something needs to be designed at all.

Still, there is opportunity hidden in that tension. The pressure designers feel creates space for reflection: why are certain forms of design losing their appeal? What do these moral boundaries say about our time? And what’s at stake if everything has to be ‘right’?

Some designers choose to stop making altogether and focus solely on research and analysis. Others feel a strong need to create something tangible in an increasingly digital world — or dive deep into digital immersion, in search of new forms of experience and meaning.

Design doesn't have to only follow. It can also mirror, question, and surprise. By entering the conversation about the boundaries we feel — and perhaps even impose ourselves — space opens up. For new ideas. For different perspectives.

BEING RESPONSIBLE DOESN'T MEAN WALKING ON EGGSHELLS.

DESIGNING FOR ABUNDANCE, NOT SCARCITY

Humans evolved in a world where scarcity was the rule. Sugar was rare—so when we stumbled upon honey, we devoured it with joy. A rare delight. Fast forward to today: sugar is everywhere, all the time, and this abundance is now making us sick and fat. The same goes for meat—once a celebration after a successful hunt, now mass-produced, over-consumed, and deeply problematic for our health and the planet.

This shift reveals a core human challenge: we are biologically wired for scarcity, but we live in an age of abundance. And we're struggling to adapt.

That's where design comes in.

Instead of focusing only on restriction and control, we must design new systems, spaces, and experiences that help us live wisely within abundance. Not to go back to simpler times, but to reimagine our future-forward habitats—where technology and ecology work together, not against each other.

How can we shape a world where abundance fuels wellbeing rather than excess? What does a future of designed self-restraint, joyful sustainability, and mindful interaction look like?

Let's move from surviving scarcity to thriving in abundance.

FREEDOM FOR DESIGN

6 principles

DO YOU
☐ AGREE
OR
☐ DISAGREE
WITH THESE
PRICIPLES?

LET'S START
THE DEBATE

Instead of reducing design to an extension of policy or a rigid framework of generic social responsibility, we advocate for a future where design once again serves the unthinkable, the unexpected, and the not-yet-existent.

Designers must be given space for friction, play, and wonder. No longer driven by duty, but by curiosity. Not bound by what must be done, but inspired by what could be.

That's why we present the following principles—as an invitation to redesign design itself.

NO FREEDOM, NO CREATIVITY

When designers are limited in by what is socially expected or deemed appropriate, the space for surprise, imagination, and radical innovation disappears. What we get instead are safe, tame designs that comfort more than they challenge. Freedom is the oxygen of creativity. Only when designers are free to explore the uncomfortable—without fear or judgment—can true innovation emerge.

2

RESPONSIBILITY SHOULD EMPOWER, NOT CONSTRAIN

Imposing responsibility can put designers under constant pressure to make moral and ethical judgments. This so-called "responsible" approach can be paralyzing. Openness means that designers don't always need to frame their thinking in terms of right and wrong. Don't keep asking: is this good? Instead, ask: does it work? Does it do what it promises to do?

3

KEEP DESIGN INDEPENDENT

Design can only truly innovate when designers have the freedom to make their own choices. When design becomes too subservient to abstract societal transition processes, it loses its intrinsic value. Independence – the autonomy to choose one's own relationships and directions – gives designers the space to work from their own strength and vision.

4

BRING BEAUTY BACK

Design isn't just about solving problems — it also brings beauty, joy, and a sense of humanity into our everyday lives. It can improve quality of life by putting aesthetics, comfort, creativity, and happiness at the center. Beauty doesn't always need to be functional; sometimes it simply moves you — because it touches, surprises, or inspires and wonder.

5

FREEDOM NURTURES DIVERSITY

When designers are freed from narrow definitions of social responsibility at large, space opens up for diverse approaches. Some might focus on innovation, others on beauty, technology, or something completely unexpected. That diversity makes the design field stronger. We often assume that 'responsible' projects make the world a better place—but that doesn't mean other ideas are any less valuable.

6

FACILITATE, DO NOT DICTATE

Designers can make suggestions, but the final choice lies with the user, the client, and the citizen. People should be empowered to make conscious decisions about how they use products and services. Design should facilitate, not dictate. Kill the little priest in you.

Large art and design events serve significant economic and cultural interests but also contribute to mass tourism, pollution, and rising living costs.

At the same time, these events provide important platforms to address these issues, offering designers the opportunity to explore how things can be done differently and more sustainably.

Newsletter The New Institute Rotterdam

Not everything that grows needs to be controlled.

Sometimes, beauty emerges precisely through freedom and chaos.

Koert van Mensvoort

THE NO DESIGN MANIFESTO

This text is a slogan-style summary of the piece
FREEDOM for DESIGN
THE NO DESIGN MANIFESTO,
written by Silvio Lorusso, Geert Lovink,
Ned Rossiter and Mieke Gerritzen.

WHEN ETHICS BECOME BRANDING, CREATIVITY DISAPPEARS.

FROM DO-GOOD TO DO-BETTER: ETHICS NEED AN UPDATE!

COOL DESIGN ONCE SOLD MORE STUFF.

TIME TO DESIGN LESS, BUT MEAN MORE.

CREATIVITY SHRINKS WHEN MARKETS SET THE RULES.

DESIGNERS AREN'T TOOLS.

DON'T TREAT THEM LIKE ONE.

DESIGN WON'T SAVE THE WORLD.

UNLESS IT DARES TO QUESTION IT.

IM PASSE PAR TOUT

NO MORE MAKERS

WE CRAVE AUTHENTICITY, BUT BUY ILLUSIONS.

RENDER STRATEGIES
DISCOVER INNOVATION
CHANNEL DIVERSITY
DESIGN IMPACT
FILTER IDEAS
CO-CREATE HOPE
PROTOTYPE CHANGE
MODEL WORLDS
CATALYZE BUSINESSES
SANDBOX SENSATIONS
PILOT FUTURES
REWILD IMAGINATION
RECYCLE VISION
SKILLS EXPIRE

HANDMADE STORIES, MASS-PRODUCED TRUTHS.

DESIGN IS MORE THAN A MOODBOARD FOR THE SMART CITY.

IF EVERYTHING IS 'REAL', WHY DOES IT FEEL SO FAKE?

DON'T PROTOTYPE THE FUTURE— QUESTION WHO'S WRITING IT.

THE SYSTEM ISN'T DEAD —IT JUST CHANGED OUTFITS.

JUST SAY NO!

DESIGNERS KNOW BEFORE THE SYSTEM DOES.

THAT'S OUR SECRET.

THE CREATIVE INDUSTRY IS A WICKED PROBLEM IN ITSELF.

DON'T CONFUSE SCALE WITH RELEVANCE. SMALL CAN BE RADICAL.

FOLLOW THE MONEY, SURE— BUT NEVER TRUST IT.

DESIGN IS BECOMING A LUXURY HOBBY FOR THE RICH.

POVERTY SUCKS

There is no true creativity without freedom. Anything less is subpar, consumerist, and for the purchase of vapid billionaires and oligarchs.

Badiucao

SKILLS EXPIRE. AESTHETICS SURVIVE–SOMETIMES.

PRECARITY BY DESIGN: WELCOME TO THE POVERTY OF WASTE.

GRADUATE INTO THE GLOW OF ANIMATED BRANDS— OR DISAPPEAR INSIDE THE MACHINE.

THE SCRIPT WON'T SAVE YOU. TRASH IT. RECYCLE IT. REINVENT IT.

IN A SYSTEM ALLERGIC TO CRITIQUE, COLLECTIVES REMAIN THE LAST GLITCH.

DESIGN IS NEVER NEUTRAL— CHOOSE YOUR SIDE.

WAR DESIGN

DESIGN IS STRATEGY. USE IT TO RESIST, NOT TO COMPLY.

BETWEEN POWER AND THE PEOPLE, DESIGN IS THE FRONTLINE.

GUILT IS NOT A DESIGN STRATEGY.

A CULTURE OF SHAME AND GUILT

DESIGN WON'T SAVE THE WORLD IF IT'S BUSY BEGGING FOR FORGIVE-NESS.

MORAL PANIC IS NOT A BLUEPRINT.

FORGET THE MANIFESTO. DESIGN SOMETHING THAT SPEAKS FOR ITSELF.

DESIGNERS, STOP APOLOGIZING AND START IMAGINING.

DISCIPLINE OR DISCIPLINING?

DESIGN AT A CROSS-ROAD

NO VISION WITHOUT REBELLION. NO FUTURE WITHOUT FRICTION.

THE SUPEREGO TEACHES GUILT. DESIGN TEACHES IMAGINATION.

DON'T DECORATE THE CRISIS.

ESCAPE THE MANAGERIAL MAZE – DESIGN YOUR OWN EXODUS.

LESS
ETHICS
MORE
POLITICS

DESIGN SHAME

CREATE FROM WITHIN, NOT FROM ABOVE.

CREATIVITY IS NOT A CHECKLIST. IT'S A LIVING ORGANISM. FEED IT FREEDOM.

NO ETHICS WITHOUT POLITICS

WHEN ETHICS BECOME CODE, DESIGN BECOMES CAPTIVE. BREAK THE LOOP.

TIME FOR META ETHICS

THANKS BUT NO THANKS

DON'T JUST DESIGN FOR RULES – DESIGN FOR REVOLUTION.

WE DON'T NEED MORE WARNINGS. WE NEED NEW WORLDS.

DESIGN SHOULDN'T GUILT US INTO ACTION – IT SHOULD TEMPT US FORWARD.

WHAT DESIGN CAN'T DO

Book title, Silvio Lorusso

IMPACT CIRCULARITY TRANSITION AND ECOSYSTEM

YOU STAYED HOME. THE EMPTY PLANES FLEW ANYWAY.

WHAT? YOU STILL FLY?

WE DESIGN FOR SUSTAIN-ABILITY—BUT IS HUMANITY STILL WORTH SAVING?

FIRST WE BROKE THE PLANET, NOW WE PREACH ABOUT FIXING IT. HOW CONVENIENT.

BAD IDEAS

DESIGN ONCE SHAPED THE FUTURE. NOW IT BEGS FOR FORGIVENESS.

FROM CLIMATE SINNER TO SUSTAINABI-LITY SAINT: THE DESIGNER'S REDEMPTION ARC IS FULLY FUNDED.

DESIGN SHAPED THE 20TH CENTURY. WILL IT DARE TO QUESTION THE 21ST?

DESIGNS ROLE IN CURRENT CRISIS

IN THE AGE OF ECO-GUILT AND MOSSY MANIFESTOS, WHO DARES TO DESIGN WITHOUT SHAME?

BETWEEN BIG TECH AND BIG GUILT, DESIGN MUST FIND A NEW ATTITUDE – OR BE DESIGNED OUT.

NO PERMISSION NEEDED. NO POLICY REQUIRED. JUST DESIGN THE DAMN ALTERNATIVE.

RECLAIM FREEDOM

SAY NO

STAY WEIRD, START SOMETHING.

SAY NO

NO MAP, NO MANDATE, JUST MOMENTUM.

SAY NO

WALK OUT OF THE MEETING. INTO THE UNKNOWN.

SAY NO

DON'T ALIGN.
DON'T
COMPLY.
DESIGN.

SAY NO

BUILD YOUR OWN PLATFORM.

SAY NO TO BUSINESS-AS-USUAL. SAY YES TO PLANETARY IMAGINATION.

Read the full text,
FREEDOM for DESIGN
THE NO DESIGN MANIFESTO,
written by Silvio Lorusso,
Geert Lovink, Ned Rossiter
and Mieke Gerritzen at
networkcultures.org

WE CAN'T SOLVE PROBLEMS BY USING THE SAME KIND OF THINKING WE USED WHEN WE CREATED THEM.

Albert Einstein

NO WORDS:
TRUMP'S FORBIDDEN WORDS 2025

HOW DID WE GET HERE?

Activism, activists, advocacy, advocate, advocates, barrier, barriers, biased, biased toward biases, bipoc, black and latinx, community diversity, community equity, cultural differences, cultural heritage, culturally responsive, disabilities, disability, discriminated, discrimination, discriminatory, diverse backgrounds, diverse communities, diverse community, diverse group, diverse groups, diversified, diversify, diversifying, diversity and inclusion, diversity equity, enhance the diversity, enhancing diversity, equal opportunity, equality, equitable, equity, ethnicity, excluded, female, females, fostering inclusivity, gender, gender diversity, genders, hate speech,hispanic minority, historically, implicit bias, implicit biases, inclusion, inclusive, inclusiveness, inclusivity, increase diversity, increase the diversity, indigenous community, inequalities, inequality, inequitable, inequities, institutional, lgbtqia+, marginalize, marginalized, minorities, minority, multicultural, polarization, political, prejudice, privileges, promoting diversity, race and ethnicity, racial, racial diversity, racial inequality, racial justice, racially, racism, sense of belonging, sexual preferences, social justice, sociocultural, socioeconomic, status, stereotypes, [illegible] trauma, under appreciated, [illegible]sented, under served, [illegible]sentation.

Part

2

NO What?

PART 2

No Meat
No Milk
No Alcohol
No Sugar
No White Flour
No Calories
No Sitting
No Skiing
No Flowers
No BBQ/Campfire
No Flying
No Babies
No Smoking
No Fast Fashion
No Phones
No Tiktok
No Platforms

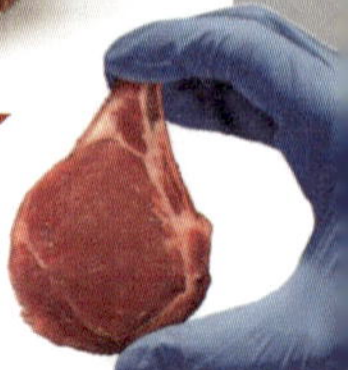

NO MEAT

NO MISTEAK
LET IT BEEF
POULETTEKES

Product titles of the Vegetarische Slager, Dutch vegetarian butcher

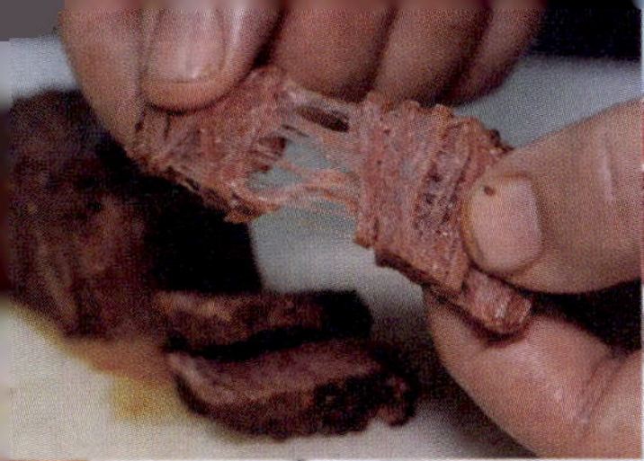

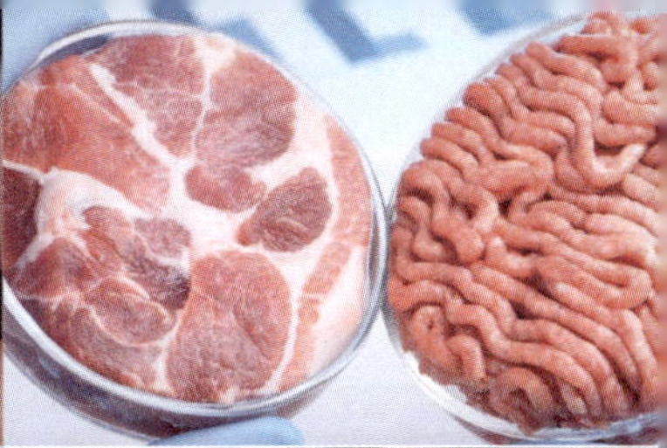

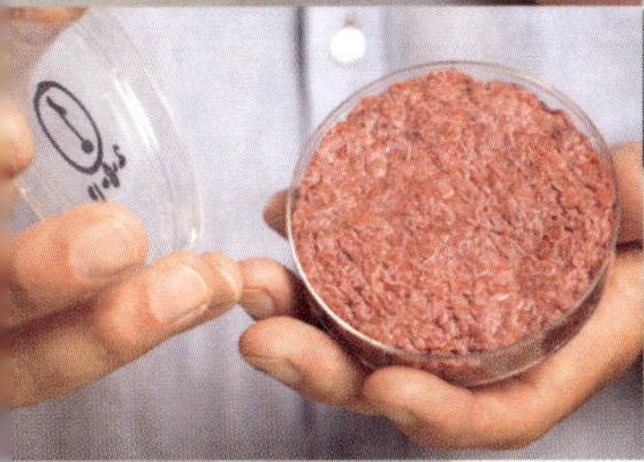

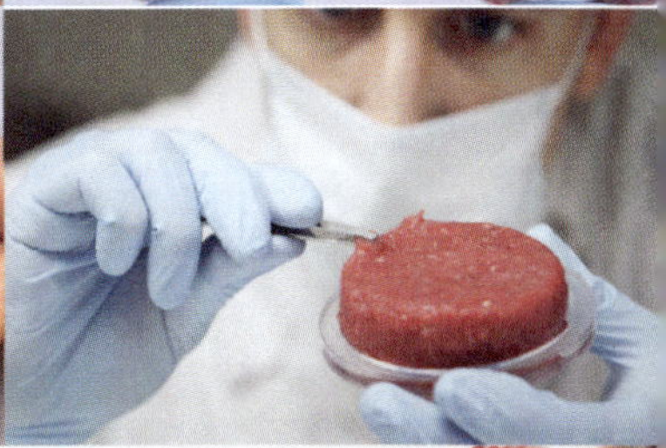

Printed and lab-grown meat are design challenges because they shape not just taste and texture, but also ethics, experience, and acceptance. It's not just about producing food, but about redesigning our relationship with animals and our food culture. Lab-grown meat is accepted in Singapore, US and Isreal.

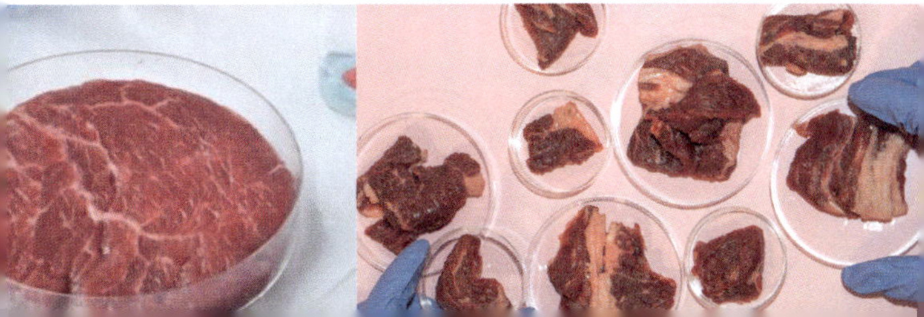

IT'S NOT *NOT* DRINKING

NO ALCOHOL

Bavaria

Cheers or no cheers?

Designated Driver?

STYLE & FINISH

Syrah grapes from the Languedoc region of France, with a silky, well-balanced, lively, and rather dry finish

OPP #56:
Todd White
Dry Farm Wines

PALEO & KETO-FRIENDLY HEALTHY WINES WITH ZERO SUGAR, CHEMICALS OR HANGOVER

OPTIMAL PERFORMANCE

Heineken 0.0

When dieting or not.

The market for alcohol-free drinks has grown significantly, especially among millennials, reflecting a shift toward healthier lifestyles.
Design your own behavior toward a more conscious way of living — with stylish alternatives.

ineken 0.0
When driving or not.

While milk is a nutritious and easily digestible product for some, it is not essential for everyone.

Vegetarische Slager, Dutch vegetarian butcher

De havermelkelite

Hoe de nieuwe yup de stad onherkenbaar verandert

THE ORIGINAL
OAT-
LY!

"Fat-free" and "sugar-free" products promise health but often deliver the opposite. Stripped of natural ingredients, they're filled with artificial sweeteners, fillers, and chemicals to mimic taste and texture. It's not nutrition — it's marketing.

GAR 0% FREE

MAYO ZERO

Fat Free MAYO

0g of Fat per Serving & Cholesterol Free

Chocolate Meringues

Sugar Free

35 Calories per serving

Keto Friendly

Gluten Free • Fat Free

WHAT DOES COKE ZERO SUGAR TASTE LIKE?

SKINNY FOOD CO.

zero calorie

LIGHTER THAN LIGHT MAYONNAISE

15CALS PER TABLESPOON

NOSUGAR COMPANY

1 MONTH OF SUGAR-FREE SNACKS

GRAIN

Heart HEALTHY

Nature's Own Life

100% WHOLE GRAIN

too good

ZERO SUGAR

0

NO WHITE FLOUR

White flour products like bread and pasta are cheap, shelf-stable, and profitable — designed to sell, not to nourish. Stripped of fiber and nutrients, they spike blood sugar, fuel cravings, and drive repeat consumption. A perfect product in a system that values profit over health.

NO CALORIES

Ozempic shows how technology is redesigning the human body — not through natural evolution, but through self-directed biochemical optimization. It's self-design in its purest form: a pill against desire, shaping our bodies and identities in a world driven by abundance.

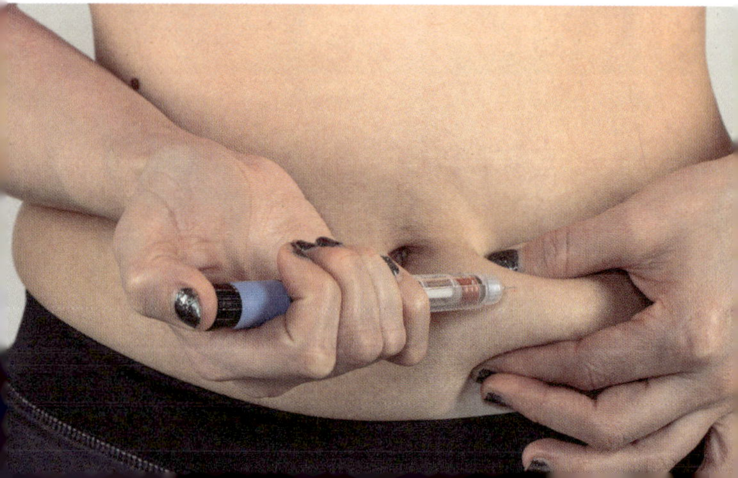

As GLP-1 drugs like Wegovy, Mounjaro and Ozempic become more popular, the widespread use of these appetite-suppressing medications is having an impact on supermarket spending, a recent study finds.

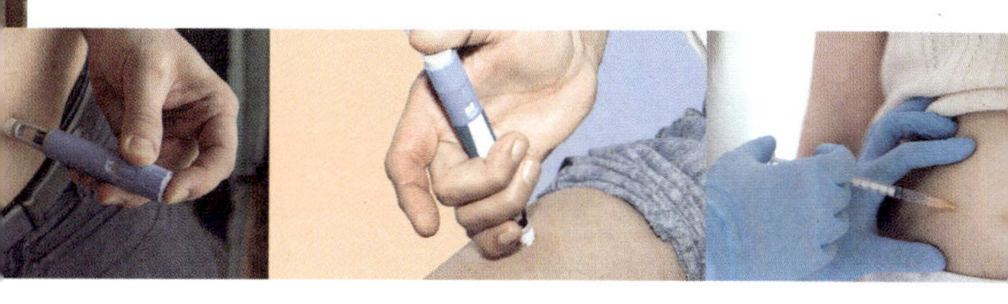

IN 2024, ± 15.5 MILLION PEOPLE USED WEIGHT-LOSS INJECTIONS.

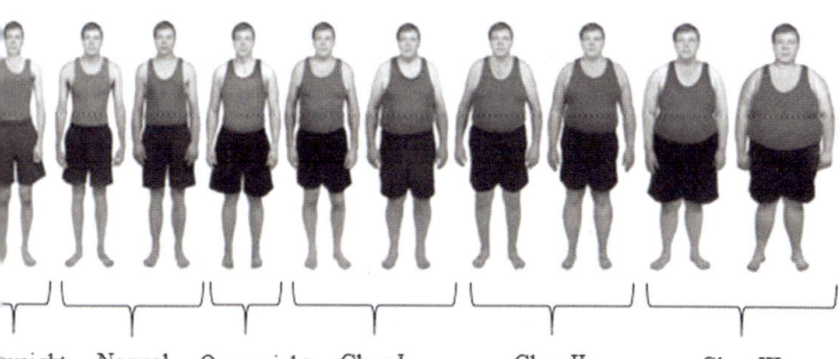

NO SITTING

THE END OF SITTING, Barbara Visser and studio RAAAF

Sitting for long periods slows circulation, weakens muscles, and increases the risk of diabetes, heart disease, and back problems. Even if you exercise, too much sitting remains unhealthy. The human body is built to move, not to stay still.

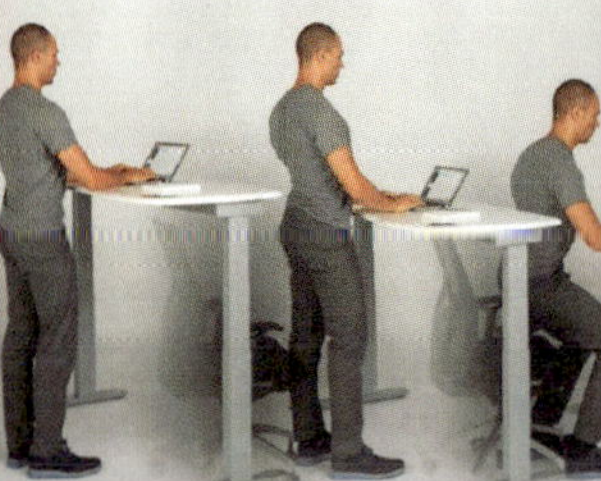

BIONIC CHAIR, Govert Flint

NO SKIING

Skiing harms the environment through artificial snow, lifts, and travel, leading to high emissions and water use. As slopes melt, resorts disrupt fragile landscapes. Even artificial grass skiing relies on plastic and energy. What was once winter fun is now an unsustainable luxury.

Olafur Eliasson's Ice Watch installation, 2018

NO FLOWERS
ON THE TABLE

Flowers may seem like a thoughtful gesture, but they often harm the environment. They require lots of water, are flown in from far, and are treated with pesticides. Cut flowers wilt quickly and offer little to a sustainable lifestyle. Choose dried flowers, or local, seasonal alternatives instead.

NO BBQ/ CAMPFIRE

Design once embraced the campfire and BBQ as icons of warmth and ritual. Today, they clash with ecological realities. Designers must rethink how we gather — creating new, low-impact rituals that honor connection without harming the planet. Warmth, redesigned for tomorrow.

ire Safe ... Fire Smart
ire Safety & Preparedness
for
ild Care, Preschool, & School-Age Child Care Programs
(Version 4)
SUN OVEN

NO FLYING

Flying symbolizes freedom — but at a high climate cost. In a changing world, real progress means traveling smarter, not faster. Choose trains, virtual meetings, and local living.

Vertrek
Departures
2

NO BABIES
EVIDENCE OVER IGNORANCE
OUR HOUSE IS ON FIRE!
SYSTEM CHANGE NOT CLIMATE CHANGE!
MAKE COOL AGAIN
PRESERVE AND CHERISH
NO BIRTHS
RECYCLE! AND SAVE our future!
DON'T MAKE GAS MASK FOR — NEW BORN BABIES
AIR POLLUTION
ABORTION IS HEALTHCARE
OUR FUTURE
WE WILL GO TO SCHOOL IF YOU KEEP THE CLIMATE COOL!

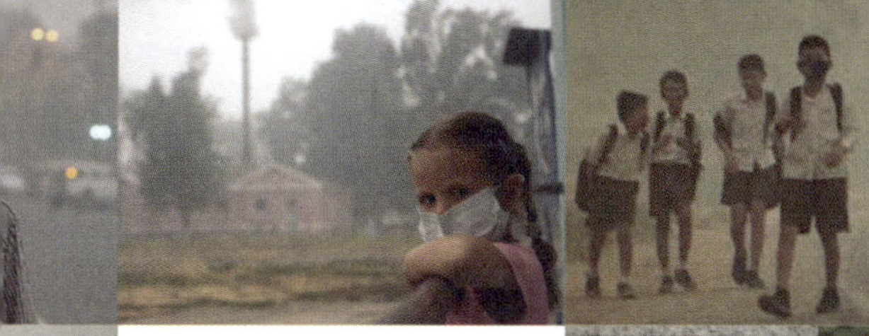

WHAT ABOUT THE CHILDREN?

NO SMOKING

Vaping attracts youth as a sleek, tech-forward upgrade — with playful colors, smooth packaging, and gadget-like design — while delivering the same harm as cigarettes. As nature and tech blur, design makes danger feel clean, futuristic, even cool.

Magic Dragon

NO FAST FASHION

Designers can contribute to a healthier fashion world by designing with longevity, adaptability, and reuse in mind. They can work with circular materials, create modular designs, focus on timeless aesthetics, and develop systems in which clothing is taken back, repaired, or upcycled.

Photo: The Revival.

NO PHONES

NO TIKTOK

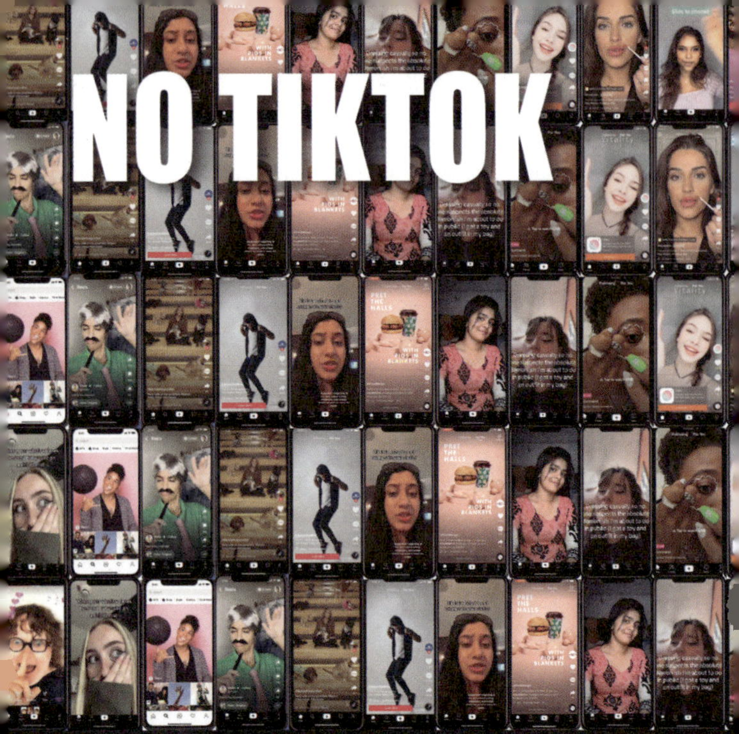

TikTok isn't a creative platform — it's a behavior machine that steers attention, rewards imitation, and dulls originality through algorithmic feedback loops.

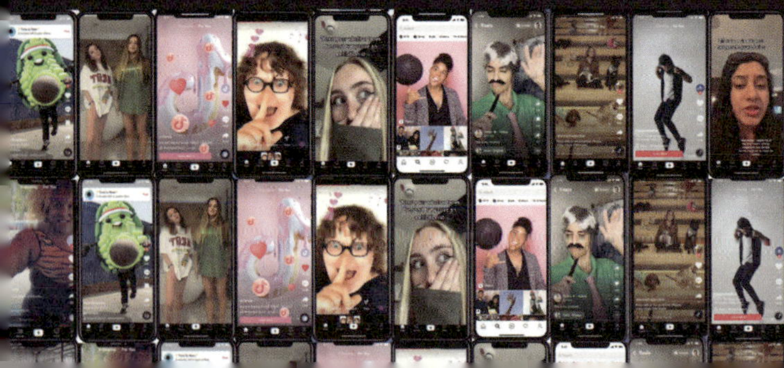

NO PLATFORM
Facebook
Instagram
X
Telegram
Threads
YouTube
Skype

Design shouldn't manipulate, but empower — by making platforms clear, fair, and built for people, not just profit.

Part

3

What do others say?

AIWEN YIN
CHLOÉ RUTZERVELD
CAROLYN STRAUSS
EDWIN GARDNER
EMMA VAN DER LEEST
GEERT LOVINK
GIULIO FRIGIERI
HENDRIK-JAN GRIEVINK
JURIAN STRIK
LIDEWIJ EDELKOORT
LUNA MAURER
MARLEEN STIKKER
MARIA CHRISTINA DIDERO
MIKE MONTEIRO
MIRIAM VAN DER LUBBE
NERI OXMAN & LEX FRIDMAN
NOOR VAN EEKELEN
PAOLA ANTONELLI
PETER LUNENFELD
ROOSJE KLAP

AIWEN YIN

Practicing Designer, Theorist and project developer

In an era of ethical disorientation, we must design practical new ways of organizing. But beyond the designs themselves, we urgently need supportive environments for experimentation, reflection, and failure — free from the paralyzing fear of accusation and cancellation.

More info: linkedin.com/in/aiwen-yin-a1525231/

CHLOË RUTZERVELD

Critical Food Designer

If you're determined to keep eating meat, are you also willing to grow it yourself — from your own cells, nourished by your own body?

"Suddenly, the vegetarian appears to be the true hedonist."

Source: De Bioreactor Amulet, In Vitro Me (2013)
chloerutzerveld.com/in-vitro-me

CAROLYN STRAUSS

Writer and founder of Slow Research Lab

Humans can perceive only a tiny fraction of what goes on in the world around us. Given this deficit, it seems foolish to wage our bets solely on what is 'known.' Opening ourselves instead to the potencies of the unknown—both within and without—is the key to unlocking alternative design futures.

More information: slowlab.net

EDWIN GARDNER

Chrononaut, Future thinker and Co-founder & Director - Studio Monnik

The future, like the past, is another culture. Shaped by ideas, identities and behaviours that might feel strange to you. Culture shock is thus inevitable when doing time travel. But the good thing is – what culture shock teaches you – is that cultures are man-made constructions, evolving to meet the epistemological and technological requirements of the moment.

We should all strive to be part of that process of culturing – infusing it with more positive vibes and open-minded curiosity, healing and gratitude.

More information: monnik.org

EMMA VAN DER LEEST

Biodesigner | researcher

Biodesign incorporates living organisms — such as bacteria, fungi, algae, or cells — into the design process.

It operates at the intersection of science and sustainability, focusing on natural materials, circular innovation, and connecting disciplines from design to science and business, both locally and globally. This is how we create materials that support biodiversity, inclusion, and future generations — and help build a just, ecological, and shared future.

More information: emmavanderleest.com

GEERT LOVINK

Media theorist | internet critic | writer

I don't want to talk about 'ethics', as the term has recently been so compromised in the context of AI.

More information: networkcultures.org

GIULIO FRIGIERI FRSA, FRGS
Writer | consultant Governance of AI | Data by Design.

Many designers feel pressured to have an opinion about AI, but the core question isn't whether we are for or against it — it's about our responsibility in shaping AI. Not just as a technology, but as a system with societal impact. Design must help create ethical frameworks and conditions — while we still can.

Design as Mapping. Leadership and Value Creation in Digital Governance. Linkedin.com

HENDRIK-JAN GRIEVINK

Artist | Designer | Researcher

To have Technology Privilege means being confident that the systems are built to serve you — not to be weaponized against you.

TO DESIGN IS TO RESPOND.

The depth of our perception determines the quality of that response. That's why we need Deep Tools — to help us see, feel and act with greater clarity and higher consciousness. Might AI become a companion in that pursuit?

More info: linkedin.com/in/hendrikjangrievink/

LIDEWIJ EDELKOORT

Dutch Trend Forcaster

The only shame is in more of the same.

Marketing and tiktokking are strangling possible outcomes to be all similar and in zinc with millions of followers. In a world filled with stuff we make even more stuff until we become insensible to a new aesthetic call. Therefore, the abstraction of abstinence and fasting of fashion might bring a relieve of consumption.

More information: edelkoort.com

JURIAN STRIK

Creative Strategist | Designer | Program Maker

SHAME IS NOT THE GAME.

Be kind as neighbour,
elusive as consumer,
switched-on as citizen,
unquantifiable as clickfarm,
gentle as earth dweller,
mortal as the lump of flesh you
are fierce as lover and friend,
and all of the above as a

DESIGNER.

More information: strik.com

LUNA MAURER

Interaction and media design artist

Designing friction instead of removing it is the task for a new generation of technology developers.

Friction is uncomfortable, rough, slows things down, makes boundaries felt, engages the body, is sometimes difficult – and above all: unpredictable. But it is precisely these qualities that form a fundamental part of being human. Friction is the human experience that refuses to be optimized away.

In our surveillance society, data and transparency are the greatest forms of capital. Privacy has become a privilege for the few.
Byung Chul-Han states: transparency means exposure, exhaustion, burnout.
Shame and distance cannot be integrated into the accelerated circulations of capital, information, and communication. As a result, our world is becoming increasingly shameless and bare.

More information: lunamaurer.com/

MARLEEN STIKKER

Director of Waag Society/Futurelab

We need to regain our sovereignty and self-determination in our lives and societies. To achieve that, it's crucial that we don't accept black box technology anymore, but create and use alternatives that put our freedoms at the core.

Source: Marleen Stikker, keynote LibrePlanet 2022

MARIA CRISTINA DIDERO

Italian curator | historian | author | design scholar

Design
is all about
people,
not about
chairs.

Source: Wikipedia.org

MIKE MONTEIRO

Writer of the book Ruined by Design

You are responsible for what you put into the world. And you are responsible for the effects those things have upon the world.

Source: Ruined by Design: How Designers Destroyed the World, and What We Can Do to Fix It.

MIRIAM VAN DER LUBBE

Designer | Creative Head Dutch Design Week

I'm convinced that aesthetics are a prerequisite for impact — they open the door to meaning. Beauty for beauty's sake is complicated, because who decides what's beautiful? But if something lacks appeal, it also loses the invitation to look closer and discover what the design is really about. At Dutch Design Week, we deeply value that kind of substance — the idea that design should truly contribute to shaping the future. Younger generations especially understand that we are all co-designing the world we live in. Creating something is never separate from that world, or from the choices you make: the materials you use, the people you collaborate with, and the impact your design has. But moving people emotionally — that too is a powerful value in design.

Source: Design as a Moral Act
ddw.nl/nl/nieuws/896/design-as-a-moral-act

NERI OXMAN EN LEX FRIDMAN

Neri Oxman is a designer | engineer | scientist, and artist. Lex Fridman is an American computer scientist | podcaster

Lex Fridman: So beyond genes and evolution, if there was a way to augment nature and allow it access to the world of bits, what does nature look like now?

Neri Oxman: Obviously with responsibility, obviously with control, obviously with ethics and moral code, but is there a world in which nature can help fix itself using those tools?

This dialogue highlights Oxman's vision of a future in which designers and technological innovations collaborate with nature, rather than exploit it, aiming to create a more sustainable and ethically responsible world.

Source: Excerpt from Podcast (#394)
youtube.com/shorts/ak8_0XmygWA

NOOR VAN EEKELEN

Designer | Creative Lead Next Nature

Design requires boldness. Not validation.

bbbb

More information: nextnature.org

PAOLA ANTONELLI

Italian architect | curator | author | the Senior Curator of Architecture and Design at the MoMA

Design doesn't always make the world a better place. *Amen*.

"Although it took me a while to understand that. Perhaps because I am the daughter of doctors, I thought that designers took a kind of Hippocratic oath and worked for the good of humanity. In 2012, plans for 3D printed firearms were distributed and I had an epiphany: in the hands of humans, any tool can be used for evil."

Source: El País

PETER LUNENFELD

American Writer | Professor Design Media Art UCLA

The future only exists in our imaginations, so any design ethic must include taking on the future as a client. As designers are those rare humans who can make their dreams manifest as images, objects, and systems, they must hallucinate a world they actually want to live in.

More information: peterlunenfeld.com

ROOSJE KLAP

Designer | Scientist | Curator | Educator

Each time I use computational
power to make stories visible,
I feel shame drawing heat from
rivers to cool our datacenters,
from deadly silencing landscapes,
and its lives we do not hear.

Is it even possible to stop
giving shape to control, and
enable other narratives —
reminding us how to live 'with,'
not 'over;' wind, stone,
creature and leaf?

None of it ours to own,
only to honor?

More information: ark.amsterdam/

LET'S NOT DIVIDE DESIGN INTO OPPOSING CAMPS.

AFTERWORD - BETWEEN THINKING AND MAKING

In recent years, there has been a growing focus on design criticism, especially within art and design education. Designers are increasingly moving away from simply creating products and are instead engaging with research, reflection, and pressing societal themes. In a world full of complexity — and shelves full of stuff — that shift makes sense. Design is more than making: it is a way to think about the world, about how we live together, and where we might be heading.

At the same time, we see an interesting shift within the field: from making to thinking, from material to concept. Some even speak of a division — between design as an industrial craft and design as a philosophical or societal practice. Both approaches are valuable, but it's clear that physical making has, at times, taken a back seat. Craftsmanship, material sensitivity, and aesthetics are receiving less attention, even though they are essential to what makes design powerful.

This development is understandable. Conceptual thinking and research tend to receive recognition more quickly — academically or socially — than the slower, often uncertain process of creating something that both functions and resonates. Design connects well to urgent topics such as ecology, justice, and technology — subjects that invite analysis, language, and strategy. But there's a risk in this abstraction: that the tactile, visual, and experiential aspects of design are taken less seriously. That the final product is presented as an afterthought, rather than the heart of the work.

And yet, this shift also opens up opportunities. We live in a world where systems and technology increasingly shape our relationships and experiences. That's exactly why we must not lose sight of the physical and the human. We are still here — with bodies, senses, and emotions. Even as design becomes more idea-driven, it remains something we touch, use, and experience.

The rise of design criticism shows a maturing of the discipline. It signals a departure from pure styling and a deeper engagement with the questions of our time. And that is something to celebrate. Design as a critical field is a valuable addition to the academy – and far beyond it.

But let's not forget where the true power of design lies: in the union of head and hand. Thinking and making don't cancel each other out – they strengthen each other. Reflection enriches the work, while the act of making generates new insights. The challenge is to avoid getting stuck in abstraction, without falling into thoughtless production. When designers manage to combine both worlds, they create space for work that resonates – in thought and in form.

Everyone can talk
Few create what truly matters
Thinking is safe
Making takes guts

IN A WORLD
FULL OF NEGATIVITY,
DESIGNERS NATURALLY
WANT TO CREATE
SOMETHING POSITIVE

—

BUT NOT OUT
OF SHAME.

REAL IMPACT STARTS
WITH INTENTION,
NOT GUILT.

NEVER FORGET
AESTHETICS.

CREDITS

Concept & Design	Mieke Gerritzen
Design assistant	Lydia Halders
Research	Elena De Pasquali
Production	Next Nature
Publisher	BIS Publishers
Contributions	Aiwen Yin
	Chloé Rutzerveld
	Carolyn Strauss
	Edwin Gardner
	Emma van der Leest
	Geert Lovink
	Hendrik-Jan Grievink
	Jurian Strik
	Koert van Mensvoort
	Lidewij Edelkoort
	Luna Maurer
	Marleen Stikker
	Miriam van der Lubbe
	Ned Rossiter
	Noor van Eekelen
	Peter Lunenfeld
	Roosje Klap
	Silvio Lorusso
Thanks to	Harm van Kessel
	Institute of Network Cultures
	The Revival

Mieke Gerritzen is a designer and curator, currently creative director at Next Nature Network. Until 2017, she served as director of MOTI – Museum of the Image in Breda, where she shaped the museum's artistic direction and programming. She has authored over ten books and designed more than twenty exhibitions. Gerritzen, a forward thinker, investigates how technology transforms the worlds of art, media and design.

BISPUBLISHERS

BIS Publishers
Timorplein 46
1094 CC Amsterdam
The Netherlands
bis@bispublishers.com
www.bispublishers.com

ISBN 978 90 636 9807 2

Next Nature is the story of humankind changing its world with the fruits of knowledge and technology. We are a non-profit of creatives, thinkers, educators and supporters who want to go forward – not back – to nature. Our explorations comes to life in expos, events, education, and publications. With members in 44 countries, we make worldwide impact. In our museum of the future in the Netherlands, you can experience our vision in 'real life'. Together, we create a dreamed future for all life on Earth.

Next Nature Museum
Noord Brabantlaan 1A
Eindhoven (NL)
+31 (0)40-250-46-20
office@nextnature.net
www.nextnature.org

Institute of Network Cultures (INC) is a research center in Amsterdam. It explores the intersection of digital technology, culture, and society, focusing on practices in online publishing, the digital economy, critical media theory, and activism. The INC brings together researchers, artists, designers, and theorists to examine how networks shape culture — and how they can be critically reimagined. networkcultures.org

WHERE THERE IS NO VISION, THERE IS NO HOPE.

I BOUGHT THIS BEFORE ELON WENT CRAZY.

Anti-Musk expressions reflect a form of shame about whom we choose to follow, admire, or empower through our attention and consumption.

IEAT NO MILK NO ALCOHOL NO AVOCAD
ANAS NO SOCIAL MEDIA NO NETFLIX NO
NE NO CAR DRIVING NO FLYING NO SITT
KAGE DELIVERY NO FAST FASHION NO C
NO FLOWERS NO NOISE NO CALORIES N
NO SUGAR NO SHOPPING NO FUN NO
ICROPLASTICS NO MANIFESTOS NO T
FORM NO TIKTOK NO BBQ NO WHAT'S
S NO CAR DRIVING NO SUGAR NO MEA
LCOHOL NO AVOCADO NO BANANAS NO
A NO NETFLIX NO SMARTPHONE NO CA
NO FLYING NO SITTING NO PACKAGE D
ST FASHION NO CAMPFIRES NO FLOW
E NO CALORIES NO SMOKING NO SUGA
PPING NO FUN NO BABIES NO MICROP
ANIFESTOS NO TESLA NO PLATFORM N
BQ NO WHAT'S APP NO COWS NO CAR
UGAR NO MEAT NO MILK NO ALCOHOL N
NO BANANAS NO SOCIAL MEDIA NO N
TPHONE NO CAR DRIVING NO FLYING
NO PACKAGE DELIVERY NO FAST FASH

T NO MILK NO ALCOHOL NO AVOCADO N
AS NO SOCIAL MEDIA NO NETFLIX NO SI
NO CAR DRIVING NO FLYING NO SITTIN
GE DELIVERY NO FAST FASHION NO CAM
FLOWERS NO NOISE NO CALORIES NO S
O SUGAR NO SHOPPING NO FUN NO BA
ROPLASTICS NO MANIFESTOS NO TESL
RM NO TIKTOK NO BBQ NO WHAT'S AP
NO CAR DRIVING NO SUGAR NO MEAT N
OHOL NO AVOCADO NO BANANAS NO S
NO NETFLIX NO SMARTPHONE NO CAR D
O FLYING NO SITTING NO PACKAGE DEL
T FASHION NO CAMPFIRES NO FLOWER
NO CALORIES NO SMOKING NO SUGAR N
NG NO FUN NO BABIES NO MICROPLAS
NIFESTOS NO TESLA NO PLATFORM NO T
NO WHAT'S APP NO COWS NO CAR DR
AR NO MEAT NO MILK NO ALCOHOL NO
O BANANAS NO SOCIAL MEDIA NO NET
PHONE NO CAR DRIVING NO FLYING NO
O PACKAGE DELIVERY NO FAST FASHIO

TO HELL WITH GOOD INTENTIONS

Ivan Illich